THIS BOOK IS PRESENTED TO

Brayden Hart

IT WAS GIVEN TO YOU BY

The Rogers Family

DATE

June 29, 2014

YOUR BAPTISM DAY

GOD
CALLING
— for Kids —

GOD
CALLING
for Kids

PHIL A. SMOUSE
Based on the classic devotional
edited by A. J. Russell

Published by Barbour Publishing, Inc., P.O. Box 719, Uhrichsville, Ohio 44683
www.barbourbooks.com

Our mission is to publish and distribute inspirational products offering exceptional value and biblical encouragement to the masses.

Member of the
Evangelical Christian
Publishers Association

Printed in the United States of America.
Versa Press, Inc. East Peoria, IL 61611; May 2013; D10003927

For my wonderful family,
who made it through.
And for our best friend Pete,
who made everything better.

All is well.

Greetings!

In the fall of 1932, two British women met to pray, share some time together, and write down what they thought God was saying to and through them. The result was the wonderful book, *God Calling*.

Over the years, the work of these two anonymous friends has become one of the most beloved Christian books of all time.

I've done my best to make sure the beautiful words of these two special friends speak to your children in a language they can understand so you *both* can enjoy this remarkable devotional together.

God bless!
Phil A. Smouse

1   Between the Years

Oh, My little one, trust Me! Put your hand in Mine. Let My love make everything new. I am the door between the old and the new. I will erase the mistakes of the past *forever*.

I am the light of the world.
John 8:12

2 Arms of Love

Your life is a beautiful gift to the people around you. Open your arms. Fill this good day with laughter and joy. Let My love and your happy heart lighten the load of each person you meet.

Bear one another's burdens.
Galatians 6:2 ESV

3 The Door Will Open

Why are you worried? Trust Me and be strong! I love you. I am fighting for you. *I will win.* You will see. The door will open. My dreams for you will all come true—*one day at a time.*

Those who trust in the LORD
will find new strength.
Isaiah 40:31 NLT

4

Do Not Plan

Wonderful things are happening. All is well!
There is no need to plan ahead. I will take care
of you. I am God *Almighty*. I hold this day in My
hands. You will always have everything you need.

A man's heart plans his way,
but the LORD directs his steps.
Proverbs 16:9 NKJV

5 Pass It On

Oh, My little one, don't worry about tomorrow. You will always have enough. Let your money flow freely. I never send money to those who hide it away—only to those who pass it on. Use what you need, and then give the rest away!

God will supply every need.
Philippians 4:19 ESV

6 Sharp and Ready

When you pray, *I will listen.* No dream is too big. My plans for you will all come true. So trust Me and wait. Read My word and pray. I will use you. But you must be sharp and ready.

Present yourself approved to God.
2 Timothy 2:15 NKJV

7 The Secret Pearl

Your kind words are like beautiful pearls dropped into the stillness of a lonely heart. They may lie hidden for many years. But oh, the joy when that treasure is found!

> When he discovered a pearl of great value, he sold everything he owned and bought it!
> Matthew 13:46 NLT

8 Tiny Troubles

Sometimes I do what you ask. Other times I do not. Whatever happens—*trust Me*. These tiny troubles will only last a little while. But the reward you will find in heaven will last *forever*.

> The things that cannot be seen will last forever.
> 2 Corinthians 4:18 NLV

9 No Strain

I am the Master Builder. You are My beautiful creation. I will never put more worry on you than your little heart can bear. Strain only comes when you try to serve another master. Don't let the cares of this life steal your heart from Mine.

> My yoke is easy and my burden is light.
> Matthew 11:30

10 Of Great Price

Your life is a beautiful pearl of great price. It is a gift you can give to everyone—a priceless treasure that will live in their hearts *forever*.

> For where your treasure is,
> there your heart will be also.
> Matthew 6:21

11 Love and Silence

You can tell Me *anything*. When you look for Me, *you will find Me*. But I will not shout above the noise of this foolish world. If you seek the voice of any other, I will disappear into the morning mist.

My sheep listen to my voice;
I know them, and they follow me.
John 10:27 NLT

12 Marvelous

Come. Walk with Me. Put your hand in Mine.
The path I choose may not be easy. And at times
it will be dark and hard to find. But the place
that it takes you will be mighty and *marvelous*.

Your word is a lamp to my feet
and a light for my path.
Psalm 119:105

13 Strong!

Don't let your heart be troubled. Everything will
be all right. These dark days will not last forever.
Trust Me and be strong! Let My love and kindness touch each person you meet.

I will refine them like silver and test them like gold.
Zechariah 13:9

14   For Everything

Real joy comes when you learn to thank Me for *everything*. So give thanks! Thank Me when things are good. Thank Me when everything seems to be going wrong. Share the beauty of your thankful heart with everyone you meet.

In everything give thanks.
1 Thessalonians 5:18 NKJV

15 Peace

Peace. Be still! I am working all things together for your good. Change may come. There is no need to be afraid. Your life is safe and secure here in My loving arms.

The fruit of righteousness will be peace.
Isaiah 32:17

16 Little Things

I am the Lord of the little things! No life is too small to slip through My hands. Your heart is like a fine stone set with care to create a color-ful mosaic of incredible beauty. In My Kingdom little stones play a big part.

Let all who put their trust in You be glad.
Psalm 5:11 NLV

17 Good Things

I want to give you good things. *And I will*—but you must learn to trust Me. Close the door to fear and doubt. Don't ever let them come inside. They will rust and ruin every good thing you own.

> Give, and you will receive. . . .
> The amount you give will determine
> the amount you get back.
> Luke 6:38 NLT

18 Faith Works

Faith is a gift I give freely and with great joy. Yes, you must work. Yes, you must pray. But the key to your dreams and the answer to your prayers *depends on faith*. It is the envelope that carries every prayer straight to My throne.

> We, too, have put our faith in Christ Jesus.
> Galatians 2:16

19   Good and Perfect

If you seek Me—*you will find Me*. Like a loving father on his child's birthday, I have picked out and wrapped every good gift your heart desires. Oh, how My heart will sing when you hold those heavenly treasures in your very own hands!

How much more will your Father in heaven
give good gifts to those who ask him!
Matthew 7:11

20   One with Me

You are One with Me—your heart is My *forever* home. And I am One with the Father— the maker of heaven and earth. Think about it! What more could anyone ever want?

Think about the things that are good
and worthy of praise.
Philippians 4:8 NCV

21

You Can Rest

Rejoice. Be glad! I am with you always. Once My Word is spoken, nothing can stand in its way. Like a newborn baby asleep in its mother's arms, you are safe and secure. Rest. Rest. *Rest.*

I will be glad and rejoice in you.
Psalm 9:2

22   Gray Days

Are you having a gray and dreary day? Thank Me, and the darkness will go away! When your days are filled with thanks, the clouds will part and My light will shine. But when they are not, those gray days will go on and on *forever.*

Be thankful to Him, and bless His name.
Psalm 100:4 NKJV

23   A River of Life

Joy is the pure, clean air that fills the hearts of those who live close to Me—a river of life that passes between us without sight or sound!

The joy of the Lord is your strength.
Nehemiah 8:10 ESV

24   **By Your Side**

You are like a little boat in unknown waters. Don't worry about the waves ahead. Just move forward a little step at a time. The Lord who made the seas and the salt and the storms is right here by your side.

Lord, I believe; help my unbelief!
Mark 9:24 NKJV

25   Happiness

Happiness is a strong house built on trust. Trust is the *foundation*—the part that holds up everything else. Its rooms are fitted and filled by a joyful heart that loves to spend time with Me.

> I have come that they may have life,
> and have it to the full.
> John 10:10

26   Stay Calm

Don't let your heart be troubled. Place your worries and cares into My hands, *and leave them there.* There is nothing to fear. I am working all things together for your good.

> Give all your worries and cares to God,
> for he cares about you.
> 1 Peter 5:7 NLT

27 Height of the Storm

I am with you. Throw out your worries, fears, and doubts. Let faith, hope, and love move in to take their place. My disciples thought I was asleep during the storm. They thought I had forgotten them. *But they were wrong!* Trust Me and watch what I will do!

"Take heart; it is I. Do not be afraid."
Matthew 14:22 ESV

28   Come unto Me

What do you want to be when you grow up? Do you want to be rich and famous? Do you want to win an award? Many people do. But look around you. What do they have to show for it? A happy heart? A peaceful world? No? I wonder why not?

Come to Me, all you who labor and are
heavy laden, and I will give you rest.
Matthew 11:28 NKJV

29   I Will Make a Way

Don't be afraid. I am your shield. Everything will work out fine. Call out My name. Trust Me for *everything*. I will make a way.

Wait on the Lord.
Psalm 27:14 NKJV

30   Rest

Some days are for work. Some are for play. And some are for *rest*. Take some time to rest today. Set aside your work. Turn off the noise. Open My Word. Let Me fill your weary heart and make everything fresh and new.

> I will give you rest.
> Matthew 11:28 NKJV

31   I Know the Plans

I know the plans I have for you. They are plans to help you, not to harm you. Every pain and heartache will turn out for your good—and the good of everyone around you.

> I know the plans I have for you,
> declares the LORD.
> Jeremiah 29:11

1

A New Start

Don't be afraid—rejoice and be glad! I will make
everything new. Forget about the past. The past is
gone! Turn and walk away. Start a new life. Do it
today. I love you. *I forgive you.* You are free!

If anyone is in Christ, he is a new creation;
old things have passed away; behold,
all things have become new.
2 Corinthians 5:17 NKJV

2   As I Love You

Love *everyone* as I love you. Love your best friend when he is gentle, helpful, and kind. Love your worst enemy when he is selfish, angry, and mean. This is a difficult lesson. But you have a mighty Teacher. And I will bless you when you love like Me.

Love one another. As I have loved you.
John 13:34

3   The Walls Will Fall

Why did the walls of Jericho fall? The answer is really very simple. Nothing on this earth is strong enough to stand against a heart that truly loves Me when it is filled with songs of thanks and praise!

The king's heart is in the hand of the LORD.
Proverbs 21:1

4   Learning to Walk

When earthly help is taken away *My power comes alive*! So trust Me. Learn to walk on your own. Watch what I will do! I cannot teach you to walk if you are leaning on something or someone else.

Without faith it is impossible to please God.
Hebrews 11:6

5 You Will Know

Walk with Me. I will teach you. Listen for My voice. I will speak. Life is a school, and you will have many teachers. But none of them will ever know you, or be able to help you, better than Me.

Trust in the Lord with all your heart. . .
and He shall direct your paths.
Proverbs 3:5–6 NKJV

6 My Beloved

When you seek Me, *you will find Me.* I will answer when you call. My hands are filled with everything you will ever need. But, oh, My beloved, how My heart longs to spend time with you.

Come unto me.
Matthew 11:28 KJV

7   Light Ahead

Trust Me and do not be afraid. Open your eyes!
See all the wonderful things I am doing. For now
you are walking in deep tunnel-darkness. But just
a few steps more, and you will see the light.

> They will call upon my name,
> and I will answer them.
> Zechariah 13:9 ESV

8   Trust Me Alone

I am your Lord. Do you trust Me or not? Rely
on Me for *everything*. I have not forgotten you.
Your help is coming. Patience is faith stretched
almost to the breaking point.

> Whom have I in heaven but you?
> Psalm 73:25

9   **The Voice of God**

I don't always speak with words you can hear.
Sometimes I whisper straight to your heart.

> We have received God's Spirit. . .
> so we can know the wonderful things
> God has freely given us.
> 1 Corinthians 2:12 NLT

10   **Lifeline**

I am your Savior—your lifeline—a rope of rescue
connecting your heart to Mine. Rejoice and be
glad! Your life is in My hands. No heart can be
lost when it is connected to Me.

> Your waves and breakers
> have swept over me.
> Psalm 42:7

11 Stop Struggling

I know how hard it is to wait. But you must wait. I see your heart. You feel like a little boat, lost and alone in the middle of the ocean. Put down your oars. Stop struggling to save yourself. Look up. I come to you walking on the water!

> Be strong, and let your heart take courage; wait for the Lord!
> Psalm 27:14 ESV

12 Everywhere

Trust Me. Don't be afraid. Let your heart be filled with joy! The road that lies before you is beautiful. It is filled with amazing, new things. Come. You will find Me there. You will find Me *everywhere*!

> You have turned my mourning into joyful dancing.
> Psalm 30:11 NLT

Run!

Don't stop now. Your race is almost won! Run hard, and keep on running. Starting is easy. Anyone can do it. I know you are tired. But victory is just a few steps away. So don't give up now. RUN!

I press on toward the goal to win the prize
for which God has called me.
Philippians 3:14

14   **Here with Me**

Nothing is more important than the time we spend together. Come. Open up your heart. Tell Me what you need. I will make everything new.

Better is one day in your courts
than a thousand elsewhere.
Psalm 84:10

15 Super Power

I will use you. Together we will do great things. But remember this: The world does not need a super man. It needs a *supernatural* man—a man whose power and strength come from Me alone.

Trust in the LORD.
Psalm 4:5

16 You Are My Joy

I love you. You are My joy—a beautiful, simple doer of My word—the gift of My Father as I hung on the cross. Oh, how I thank Him daily *for you*!

You gave them to me,
and they have kept your word.
John 17:6–7 NLT

17   In the Bag

A church is a lot like a brown paper lunch bag. It is filled with wonderful food to eat. *But the church is not the food!* You will find the food your soul needs when you come near to Me.

Let us not give up meeting together,
as some are in the habit of doing.
Hebrews 10:25

18   Let Me Do It

I love you. I will take care of you. You will have the help you need. Place your worries and cares in My hands. The sun, moon, and stars obey My every command. Your problems will obey them, too.

Fathers—if your children ask for bread,
do you give them a stone?
Luke 11:11 ESV

19   Endure

I love you. I am with you. Your race is almost won. The last few steps are the hardest of all. Face your problems with laughter and joy. I will never leave you or take My love away.

Endure hardship with us
like a good soldier of Christ Jesus.
2 Timothy 2:3

20   If You Will Ask

Don't worry about anything. Pray about everything! You don't have to beg. You don't need to make a deal. Just tell Me what you need. Trust that I will do it. Then thank Me when it's done.

Let your requests be made known to God.
Philippians 4:6 NKJV

21 I Will Do the Rest

I will show you the way. You don't need to see very far ahead. Just put your hand in Mine and take one step at a time. Trust Me. Let your heart be filled with peace and joy. I will do the rest.

I will teach you wisdom's ways
and lead you in straight paths.
Proverbs 4:11 ESV

22 Trust Me Always

You must learn to trust Me always. I will never fail you. Doubt is a sin. It kept the Children of Israel out of the Promised Land. Don't let it push you into the wilderness as well.

If you have faith as small as a mustard seed. . .
Luke 17:6

23 Healing

Busy hands are happy hands. And happy hands are a joy to My heart. The winter is almost past. Soon spring will come. Let its gentle breeze and warm sunshine fill your heart with light and life.

For behold, the winter is past.
Song of Solomon 2:11

24   Share It All

Open your heart and share everything. Share your love. Share your joy. Share your happy heart. Share your time, your food, your money, your prayers. Share it all and watch what I will do!

Cast your bread upon the waters,
for you will find it after many days.
Ecclesiastes 11:1 ESV

25 The Way to Win

Joy is heaven's cure for all the troubles of this selfish, silly world. No sickness, no evil, no hopeless, helpless situation—*nothing*—can stand against a thankful, happy heart that is filled with heaven's joy.

The joy of the LORD is your strength!
Nehemiah 8:10 NLT

26 Help Is on the Way

You are a child of the King. Everything I have belongs to you. Take off your rags. Put on the beautiful robes I have given you. I will never leave you or take My love away. Do you trust Me? Will you trust Me? Ask and you will receive!

Knock and the door will be opened.
Matthew 7:7

27 **Spirit Sounds**

Do you want to hear My voice? Then you must take time to pray. Like the wind moving through the trees on a quiet spring morning, *I speak softly*. So peace, be still. The more time you spend with Me, the better *everything* in your life will be.

. . .a still small voice.
1 Kings 19:12

28   Perfect Work

Do you want to stay sharp? Then you must take time to pray. A dull tool that works hard all the time will never do good work. But a sharp tool, even if it is only used a little, will do *perfect* work.

The earnest prayer of a righteous person
has great power and produces wonderful results.
James 5:16 NLT

29   Draw Near

Many people come to Me for help. Many come because they want to be wise. Many come to learn about the future. But oh, how I long for even one person to come because they love Me with all their heart.

Come unto me.
Matthew 11:28 KJV

Shower Love

1

Shower My love on everyone around you. It will move every mountain and calm every stormy sea. My Word will bring life. But, oh, how few there are who slow down long enough to hear it.

My word. . .
will not return to me empty.
Isaiah 55:11

2 Spirit Words

The words I speak are spirit and life! They are your reward for seeking Me with all your heart. Life, joy, peace, and healing are My gift. I give them to every heart that is joined to Me and Me alone.

The Spirit alone gives eternal life.
John 6:63 NLT

3 Closer to Me

Don't be afraid to fail. My power is made perfect in weakness. The closer you get to Me, the more your mistakes will hurt. But that is a good thing. Remember, when you are weak, *I am strong.*

I will boast all the more gladly of my weaknesses, so that the power of Christ may rest upon me.
2 Corinthians 12:9 ESV

4   I Cried, Too

People will hurt you. Love them anyway. Always choose to see the good in people. But remember, when I saw how disobedient my children's hearts had become—I cried, too.

As he came closer to Jerusalem
and saw the city ahead, he began to weep.
Luke 19:41 ESV

5   Fear Not!

So many hearts are filled with fear. Fear of this, fear of that, fear of everything, everywhere, all the time! I cannot live in a heart filled with fear. So fear not! *Fear is evil.* Never let it come inside.

Perfect love casts out fear.
1 John 4:18 NKJV

6   Love and Laughter

Like a garden, a heart does not bloom in one day. Hard ground must be softened before seeds can be planted. Do you know someone with a hard heart? Love and laughter are the tools that will soften that heart and make it ready to receive My love.

Other seed fell on good soil.
It came up, grew and produced a crop.
Mark 4:8

7 Surprises

What will I do today? Where will you find Me? When your heart *and your eyes* see My goodness in everything, there's no telling what wonderful thing you will find waiting just around the bend.

For you bless the godly, O Lord.
Psalm 5:12 NLT

8 Heaven on Earth

The long, cold winter is over. Spring is here at last! Throw open the windows. Let My beauty fill your heart. Spring is My servant. It brings you a message. Listen! Can you hear it? What am I trying to say?

The old life is gone; a new life has begun!
2 Corinthians 5:17 NLT

9 Never Too Small

Nothing is ever too small to matter to Me. One tiny sparrow is more beautiful than any palace of gold. One kind word means more than the speech of any king. Oh, how I love you, My beautiful little one!

I have loved you with an everlasting love.
Jeremiah 31:3

10 Waves of Joy

Your happy heart is like a tiny pebble tossed into a quiet pond. Even though that pebble is small, the ripples it makes spread out until they have covered every drop of water there is to be found.

A merry heart does good, like medicine.
Proverbs 17:22 NKJV

11 Beauty and Joy

I have filled this good world with beauty and joy. Every blossom and bloom—every butterfly and bird—is singing you a love song. Look! Can you see it? Listen! Can you hear My voice?

He has made everything beautiful in its time.
Ecclesiastes 3:11 NKJV

12 Simplify

A simple heart is a happy heart. People and things will try to fill this good day with noise and clutter. Choose the simple things instead. They are the keys that will unlock the door to happiness and joy.

Come unto me.
Matthew 11:28 KJV

13 By My Spirit

Peace! Be still. Wait for Me. Open the door to your heart. Let Me come inside. Breathe in the gentle wind of My Holy Spirit. I am everything you will ever need—or need to know!

Not by might, nor by power,
but by my Spirit, says the LORD.
Zechariah 4:6 ESV

14

My Touch

Why are you worried? I am right here by your side.
Trust Me. Wait for Me! You will find new strength.
Don't give up. Spread your wings and fly! My touch
and a willing heart make a life filled with joy!

Those who trust in the Lord will find new strength.
Isaiah 40:31 NLT

15   Your Cross

Put down your worries and fears. They are not yours to carry. They will make you like an old man, so tired from a long journey on a hot, dusty road that he can no longer see the beauty all around him.

> He took on Himself our troubles
> and carried our sorrows.
> Isaiah 53:4 NLV

16   The Secret Place

Come, My child! Come near to Me. I wait in many hearts. But, oh, how few there are who long to find Me, and run to meet Me there.

> He who dwells in the secret place of the Most High
> shall abide under the shadow of the Almighty.
> Psalm 91:1 NKJV

17 No Greater Joy

Come. Sit with Me. Rest! There is no greater joy. Yes, you are small. Yes, you need many things. But remember, *everything*—from the tiniest grain of sand to the farthest star—all of it belongs to Me.

How much more will your Father who is in heaven give good things to those who ask him!
Matthew 7:11 ESV

18 Ask Big

Your hard times are almost over. Wonderful things are on the way! So trust Me. Ask for big things—ask Me now! I am God *Almighty*. Nothing is too large or too diffficult for Me.

If you have faith as small as a mustard seed. . .
Matthew 17:20

19   Courage!

Fear not. I am with you. Trust Me! I am a God of power. I cannot fail you. I will not fail you. Take courage, My child. Let your heart be filled with joy. I love you. All is well.

> Fear not, for I am with you.
> Isaiah 41:10 NKJV

20   Help Is on the Way

Trust Me for everything. Depend on Me and *Me alone*. When you trust Me without looking to anyone or anything else, My help can and will come from anywhere and everything.

> Commit your way to the LORD,
> Trust also in Him, and He shall bring it to pass.
> Psalm 37:5 NKJV

21

All Is Well

Your road may seem long. But I am with you. And I *will* be with you every step of the way. More joy than you can imagine lies just around the bend. I love you. I will take care of you. *All is well.*

Steady my steps according to your promise.
Psalm 119:133 ESV

22 A Flower Opened

I love you. I am your very best friend. Everything I have is yours. There isn't anything you need that I cannot supply. A marigold. A morning glory. A million dollars. Nothing is too difficult for Me. So ask Me. Ask Me now. Watch what I will do!

Why do you worry?
Matthew 6:28

23 Your Heart Sings

I am the Lord. All power is Mine. Pray and keep on praying. *I will answer.* Say it until you know it—say it until you mean it—say it until your heart sings: *"All power belongs to Jesus Christ!"*

He who promised is faithful.
Hebrews 10:23

24 Follow Me

Trust Me and fear not! Don't be like the man walking through the forest who came to a river and *stopped* because he was afraid of the water, when all along there was a bridge right there by his side.

Put your trust in the LORD.
Psalm 4:5 ESV

25 Wonderful Things

I love you. I am with you. You don't ever have to be afraid. Go forward boldly. My power is yours. Wonderful things are happening. And I will be with you each step of the way.

Let us fix our eyes on Jesus,
the author and perfecter of our faith.
Hebrews 12:2

26 Tomorrow

I am here. Don't worry about tomorrow. Tomorrow has more than enough trouble of its own. Faith is built by knowing Me. And a life built on faith does not always need to know about tomorrow.

I will give them a heart to know me.
Jeremiah 24:7

27 **Go Forward**

Peace. Be still. I love you. I am God Almighty.
I made the heavens and the earth and *everything*
in them. Go forward without fear. Step into new
life. Let My love and power fill your heart with joy!

The Lord your God is with you wherever you go.
Joshua 1:9 NKJV

28 Mountains

Faith and a heart that wants to do My will are the two tools that will move mountains out of the way. But they must always, *always* go hand in hand.

> Whatever you ask in prayer,
> you will receive, if you have faith.
> Matthew 21:22 ESV

29 A Life Apart

Rise up, My little one. Open your heart. Let Me come inside. When you seek Me, *you will find Me.* And I will reward you for it. Yes, you must live in this world. But remember, like Me, *you are not of it.*

> Arise, my love, my beautiful one, and come away.
> Song of Solomon 2:10 ESV

30   **I Am with You**

You can relax. I am watching over you. Your happy, thankful heart is the key that will open the gates of heaven. Rest in My love. Know I am with you. Open your heart and let My love come pouring in.

> You shall go out in joy
> and be led forth in peace.
> Isaiah 55:12 ESV

31   **Climbing**

Yes, I know. You have been climbing a steep hill for a long time. Your legs are weak. You're beginning to stumble. But look around. See how far you've already come. Press on! The top of the hill is almost in sight.

> "Come to me, all of you who are weary and carry
> heavy burdens, and I will give you rest."
> Matthew 11:28 NKJV

1 The Son of God

Open your eyes, My little one. Look and see! I am Jesus—the Son of the living God. I was punished for the sins of all people. There on the cross, for one brief moment, My Father turned His back on Me, so He would never, ever have to turn it on you.

> He humbled himself and became obedient
> to death—even death on a cross!
> Philippians 2:8

2 The Priceless Gift

I love you. I am with you. *I forgive you.* Put on the beautiful, clean clothes of new life. They are My priceless, free gift to you. It is not what you do but *who you are* that matters most to Me.

> Old things have passed away;
> behold, all things have become new.
> 2 Corinthians 5:17 NKJV

3 Greatness

Do you want to be great? Then you must have a heart that longs to help others. Remember, the universe *and everything in it* are Mine to rule. But I lived among you as one who served.

I am among you as one who serves.
Luke 22:27 NLT

4 You Will Be, Too

I know you are not perfect. *But I love you.* You are safe and secure here in the shelter of My mighty arms. My disciple, Peter, was not changed in one day. But he was changed. And you will be, too.

And it shall come to pass that whoever calls on the name of the LORD shall be saved.
Acts 2:21 NKJV

5   A Heart at Rest

Come. Rest. I am with you. Open your heart. Know that I am here. Look up! The sky is dark and filled with stars. The noise of this busy day is finally done. Come and talk with Me.

Ask for the ancient paths, ask where the good way is, and walk in it, and you will find rest.
Jeremiah 6:16

6   Easter Joy

I have a beautiful gift for you. But look! Your hands are so busy holding the treasures of this world that there is no room left for the gift of heaven.

I know you are looking for Jesus, who was crucified. He isn't here! He is risen from the dead, just as he said.
Matthew 28:5–6 NLT

7   Calvary

New Life is My Easter gift. I spread out My arms and died so I could give it to you. Open your heart. Let Me plant the seeds of heaven there. I walked out of the grave so you could have *eternal* life!

If you love your life, you will lose it. If you give it up in this world, you will be given eternal life.
John 12:25 CEV

8   Come Out

You are a child of heaven—My beautiful chosen one. Don't be afraid. Come out into the light. Yes, you must live in this crazy, mixed-up world. But you don't ever have to be a part of its darkness.

Come out from among them
And be separate, says the Lord.
2 Corinthians 6:17 NKJV

9   Rise Up

Rise up, My little one! Come to Me! Leave sin, sadness, fear, and doubt behind, where they belong. New life is waiting. Step out into the light!

Arise, shine,
for your light has come.
Isaiah 60:1

10   Heaven

In a palace or in a stable, in a mansion or a slum, home is where the heart is. And where My heart is welcomed home, that home is heaven.

God opposes the proud
but gives grace to the humble.
James 4:6

11 Hold Your Ground

Remember, you are My child. And My children must be different. Different ways. Different lives. Different hearts. Have you been tempted to do wrong? Love your friends, but hold your ground!

Don't touch their filthy things,
and I will welcome you.
2 Corinthians 6:17 NLT

12 Help!

Don't ever be afraid to ask Me for help. I know you are not perfect. But I love you with all of My heart. The help you need is just a prayer away.

Many will see what he has done and be amazed. They will put their trust in the LORD.
Psalm 40:3 NLT

13 Gentle

Love. Laugh! Be gentle with everyone. Let your happy heart make this angry world a better place. Simple things done with kindness and care make a beautiful path that will lead others to heaven.

Let your gentleness be evident to all.
Philippians 4:5

14 Equally Connected

When My children join their hearts and pray,
I will do amazing things. But always remember—
light and darkness must not be linked together.
If you try, My power and blessing will not come.

Do not be yoked together with unbelievers.
2 Corinthians 6:14

15 Strength

You can do all things. I will give you strength—
but only when you take time to step away from
the noise of this foolish world and rest. A tired,
mixed-up heart won't help you—or anyone else.

I can do all things
because Christ gives me the strength.
Philippians 4:13 NLV

16 Love and Forgive

Love and forgive. That is the secret—the key that
unlocks every door. Love must be real. It must be
alive. For God is love. And I and My Father—just
like you and I—are One.

The Father and I are one.
John 10:30 NLT

17 The Two Joys

There are two kinds of joy. The first comes when you open your heart and let Me in. The second comes when you begin to realize that I am here—not maybe or someday, but here right now *for real*.

In Your presence is fullness of joy.
Psalm 16:11 NKJV

18 No Dark Days

God is love. When you give someone love, you give them God. There would be no dark, lonely days if My children would simply learn to love.

Dear friends, since God so loved us,
we also ought to love one another.
1 John 4:11

19 Our Love Story

You need Me. And My broken world needs you.
This is our love story. Many a tired, broken heart
will be changed into a joyful, happy heart—
because of the time you spend alone with Me.

> Whatever you ask in prayer,
> you will receive, if you have faith.
> Matthew 21:22 ESV

20 A Broken Heart

A broken heart is a lonely heart. Do you know
someone who has this terrible pain? Stand
beside them. Stay at their side until the pain and
heartache have gone away.

> Jesus understands every weakness.
> Hebrews 4:15 CEV

21

All Is Well

I am with you. You are safe in My mighty arms. Don't be afraid. Change may come. But always remember this: I am the same yesterday, today, and forever. Relax. Rest. All is well.

Jesus Christ is the same yesterday
and today and forever.
Hebrews 13:8

22 No Complaints

Trust Me, and do as I say. I will give you everything you need. Follow My commands without
question or complaint. The puzzle before you is
Mine to solve. So let go. Let Me connect the dots,
and I will make everything new.

I am overwhelmed with joy.
Isaiah 61:10

23 Too Much Talk!

So much talk. So many words! The Tower of Babel
was built by words, words, words. Does the branch
beg the vine for the food it needs to grow? No!
That food comes *naturally*, because they are one.

I am the vine; you are the branches.
John 15:5

24 **Let Me Go First**

Have you been fishing all night? Is your little boat empty? Don't get upset. Let Me go first. Come. Pick up your nets. Row back out to the deep water. This time *I* will fill your nets with fish.

They caught such a large number of fish
that their nets began to break.
Luke 5:6

25   Bless Your Enemies

Has someone been making you angry or upset? Don't try to fix them. Pray for them instead. But don't just pray that *I* would fix them or give them what they deserve. *Ask Me to bless them.*

As I have loved you,
so you must love one another.
John 13:34

26   I Will Give You Rest

"I can do all things" does not mean, "I need to do every last, little thing everyone asks me to do, every time they ask—until I am forced to beg for help from heaven because my own strength is gone."

"Come to Me, all of you who work and have heavy loads, and I will give you rest."
Matthew 11:28 NLV

27 Can You See Me?

I am here—right beside you. Can you see Me?
Can you feel the touch of My hand? Give Me
your heart. Let Me come inside. I want to open
your eyes to the beauty of heaven.

Blessed are those who have not seen
and yet have believed.
John 20:29 ESV

28 Roundabout

Up to the top of the mountains. Down into the
deepest, darkest valley. With your hand in Mine
we will find My lost sheep. We will bring My
light to places that have never seen it before.

Everything that has happened to me here
has helped to spread the Good News.
Philippians 1:12 NLT

29 Harmony and Peace

Some days will be dark. Some things will be hard. Don't get discouraged. Let your heart be filled with joy. Kindness, gentleness, harmony, and peace are the light that shines from a candle lit by heaven.

Ask, and it will be given to you;
seek, and you will find.
Matthew 7:7 ESV

30 Springtime

Your life is filled with the promise of heaven. The winter is over. Springtime is here. Open your heart. Open it like a beautiful flower. Let Me bless it and fill it with My light and My love.

He will refresh us like rain
renewing the earth in the springtime.
Hosea 6:3

1 Waiting

I love you. I will take care of you. *All is well.*
Your life is linked with the lives of many others.
So don't be afraid to wait. While you are waiting,
I am working.

Those who wait on the LORD
shall renew their strength.
Isaiah 40:31 NKJV

2   Hearts That Smile

You can relax and enjoy this good day. The sun is shining. The birds are singing. The air is clear and warm. Come. Turn your eyes to Me. Let Me fill you with joy and make your heart smile.

I have loved you with an everlasting love.
Jeremiah 31:3

3   Happy Birthday

I love you. I am alive in your heart. Everything I have is yours. Yes, people have hurt you. But you have been born again. My birthday gift is a new heart. And that heart—like Mine—can forgive.

Blessed are the poor in spirit,
for theirs is the kingdom of heaven.
Matthew 5:3 ESV

4 Tell Me Your Dreams

Trust Me and ask for big things. Reach out and take hold of everything I have promised. I spoke and the world appeared. So open up your heart. Tell Me your dreams. I can make them come true.

Faith is being sure of what we hope for
and certain of what we do not see.
Hebrews 11:1

5   **Let Me Choose**

When your dreams are My dreams, your dreams will come true. So trust Me. Take the limits off. Throw open the windows to your heart. Let Me choose the way, and then watch what I will do!

> He rewards those who seek him.
> Hebrews 11:6 ESV

6   **Dare to Trust**

Don't be afraid to touch the pain of a wounded heart. My world is broken and weary. And your heart holds the medicine the world needs. I know it isn't easy. But I am the God of the impossible.

> Let us not grow weary of doing good, for in due season we will reap, if we do not give up.
> Galatians 6:9 ESV

7 Against the Tide

Some days you can sit back and drift gently down the stream. Other days you must row, row, row your boat against the rising tide. Don't be discouraged. Pick up your oars. Let Me be the strength you need.

In quietness and trust is your strength.
Isaiah 30:15

8 At Rest

I am leading you. The road ahead is clear. Listen for My voice. Go forward without fear. Move very slowly from one task to the next. Then stop, rest, and pray. I work best when your heart is quiet.

The LORD's people
will live in peace, calm and secure.
Isaiah 32:18 CEV

9 The Music of Heaven

Things go wrong. People get angry. Friends walk away. You don't have to fix everything. You can't even if you try. So leave it all to Me. Harmony is not the music of earth. It is the music of heaven.

Never pay back evil with more evil.
Romans 12:17 NLT

10 Slow Down

Are you angry, hurried, and upset? Slow down! You are about to make a big mistake. Be still and know that I am God. Listen for My voice. Trust Me. Then do exactly what I say—and *nothing* else.

In quietness and in trust shall be your strength.
Isaiah 30:15 ESV

11   Triple-Braided

A true friend is a special gift. And a friend whose heart belongs to Me is a treasure from heaven. Two hearts that love Me is a wonderful thing. For when those two come together—I am there in power!

A triple-braided cord is not easily broken.
Ecclesiastes 4:12 NLT

12 Gladness and Joy

Fear is a thief. Doubt is a liar. Lock the doors and windows to your heart. Don't ever let fear and doubt come inside. Face the day with gladness and joy! They will protect you from each and every storm.

Call upon me in the day of trouble;
I will deliver you.
Psalm 50:15

13 Do Not Judge

Do not judge others. Every heart is different. And I alone know what lives inside. You cannot change anyone. That puzzle is too difficult, too tangled, too troubling for *anyone*—but Me.

Do not judge, and you will not be judged.
Luke 6:37

14 Here with You

I love you. I died for you. You are My friend.
You can tell Me anything, anytime, anywhere.
So come. Open up your heart. Talk with Me.
Oh, how I long to spend this day with you.

I have loved you with an everlasting love.
Jeremiah 31:3

15   Seek Me First

What are you looking for? What is the one thing your heart wants more than *anything* else? Seek My kingdom first, and all these wonderful things will be added to you as well.

Has he ever spoken and failed to act?
Has he ever promised and not carried it through?
Numbers 23:19 NLT

16   Pray and Praise

Prayer changes everything. It makes everything new. Nothing has the power to stand in its way. So pray and keep on praying. One day soon your prayers will turn into a beautiful song of praise!

Never stop praying.
1 Thessalonians 5:17 NLV

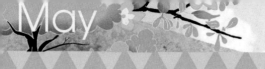

17 Sadness to Joy

Weeping may last for a night. But joy comes in the morning! My bravest little ones have learned that morning is coming—and coming soon—no matter how dark it seems right now.

Weeping may endure for a night,
But joy comes in the morning.
Psalm 30:5 NKJV

18 Look to Me

Look to Me and your worry will disappear. Look to Me and your sadness will go away. Look to Me and peace will flow into your heart like a mighty river. Look to Me *and you will be saved.*

Look to me for salvation!
For I am God; there is no other.
Isaiah 45:22 NLT

19   Your Lifeline

I know you are afraid. But trust Me and rest.
My arms are not too short to save you. Reach
out. Take hold of My Word. It is your lifeline.
Every promise you believe brings you closer to
the shore.

> The arm of the Lord is not too short to save.
> Isaiah 59:1

20   Win It All

A heart that trusts Me can never be shaken. So
rise up. Face your fears. I am with you. All is well.
Evil *must* go away. So fight to win. When you
win Me—*you win it all.*

> His right hand has won a mighty victory;
> his holy arm has shown his saving power!
> Psalm 98:1 NLT

21   At My Feet

Do you want to see Me? Then you must give Me all of your cares and worries. You must lay them at My feet and show Me a happy heart filled with joy—ready and willing to trust Me completely.

Take off your sandals, for you are standing on holy ground.
Exodus 3:5 NLT

22 Two Kinds of Trust

There are two kinds of trust. One kind knows how *and when* to wait and wait and wait. The other kind is not afraid to move quickly when the right way is ahead, and I have said, "Go!"

> You did not receive a spirit that makes you a slave again to fear.
> Romans 8:15

23 Little Worries

Little worries can cause a lot of big problems. Is your heart troubled today? Don't let your little worries pile up. Set them all down. They belong to Me. There. That's better. Now you are free.

> Give all your worries and cares to God, for he cares about you.
> 1 Peter 5:7 NLT

24 More Than Enough

I love to give more than enough. Not just a few little fish. But so many fish that your nets rip and your boat begins to sink. So remember, ask for big things. Trust Me. Then share My blessing with joy.

Put out into deep water,
and let down the nets for a catch.
Luke 5:4

25   Yes, You Can

You can do all things. I will give you strength. Don't ever give up when the going gets tough. Not every road will be easy. But that's okay. When your strength is gone, Mine is just getting started.

I can do all things through Christ
who strengthens me.
Philippians 4:13

26   Ask for More

Do you know someone who loves Me and seems to do amazing things with power and ease? It did not happen by accident. You *did not see* all of the prayer, trust, and hard work that made it possible.

Ask, and you will receive,
that your joy may be full.
John 16:24

27 Roots and Fruits

When you plant a seed, what happens? First the seed sends down a root to hold it firmly in place. Then, when it is steady and strong, it sends up a shoot to fill the world with beauty and good fruit.

The seed that fell on good soil represents those who truly hear and understand God's word.
Matthew 13:23

28   **The Test**

Do you really love Me? It's not that hard to tell.
Here is the test: Are you chasing after all of the
amazing things I can do? Or is it enough—really
enough—to simply stop and spend time with Me?

Restore to me the joy of your salvation.
Psalm 51:12

29   **Forget**

Forget about the mistakes you made yesterday.
Breathe in the blessings of this good, new day.
Your arms will never be strong enough to carry
the weight of yesterday or the worries of tomorrow.
You only need to pack for *today*.

This is the day the LORD has made.
We will rejoice and be glad in it.
Psalm 118:24

30 The Best Weapon

A joyful heart is one of the best weapons you have against the power of the enemy. No evil can stand in the presence of a happy heart filled with songs of worship and praise!

Rejoice in the Lord always.
I will say it again: Rejoice!
Philippians 4:4

31 Without Words

Pray and keep on praying. Pray with words. Pray without words. Pray with kindness, gentleness, patience, and love. Pray with your heart, your life, your thoughts, and your deeds. With all you have, with all you are, at all times, in every way—*pray*!

Pray without ceasing.
1 Thessalonians 5:17 ESV

1   Together Today

I know you're not perfect. But you never will be. So you don't need to ask Me to make you into something you're not. I love you just as you are. Why don't we spend some time together today?

Come near to God
and he will come near to you.
James 4:8

2   You Are Mine

I love you. You are Mine. Everything I have is yours. Drink My cup. Feel the happiness and joy, the sadness and pain, of those around you. Reach out. Touch their hearts. Lead them home to Me.

> Those who plant seeds of peace
> will gather what is right and good.
> James 3:18 NLV

3   With Love

Love has the power to change everything. So love *everyone* and don't hold back. Love your family. Love your friends. Love the people who hurt you. Love the people whose hearts are darkened by sin. Love them and show them how to love Me!

> The greatest of these is love.
> 1 Corinthians 13:13

On and Up

4

Beauty is work. And work means waiting. So fear not! I know the plans I have for you. You *will be* My dream come true. Be gentle with yourself. Be gentle with others. On and up. I am with you.

He will give a crown of beauty for ashes,
a joyous blessing instead of mourning.
Isaiah 61:3 NLT

5 My Tender Voice

Listen! I speak softly. Turn off the rumble and racket of this noisy, foolish world, and you will hear My tender voice.

But the LORD was not in the wind.
1 Kings 19:11

6 Needs

The weak need My strength. The strong need My kindness. The lonely need My friendship. The religious need My tender heart for those who have sinned. The sinner needs My salvation.

Lord, I believe; help my unbelief!
Mark 9:24 NKJV

7 True Beauty

True beauty comes only from heaven. Run toward it like a moth is drawn to a flame. Follow after it like a little bird runs after her mother. Drink it in like the flowers drink in sunshine!

Listen, and you will find life.
Isaiah 55:3 NLT

8 Inside Out

Many people are so busy looking for things that will make them happy on the outside that they never even notice all the wonderful things I've done to make them happy on the inside.

Letting the Spirit control your mind
leads to life and peace.
Romans 8:6 NLT

9   Jump!

Your road will have a few bumps. That's not anything to be afraid of. Lace up your shoes. Run the race I have set before you. When you come to a hurdle, don't slow down. Trust me and *jump*!

> Let us run with endurance
> the race that is set before us.
> Hebrews 12:1 ESV

10   Draw Out More

What do you need today? I have more than enough. So ask Me. Ask Me now! My well will never run dry. Take what you need for this day. Then come back tomorrow and take out more.

> Store up for yourselves treasures in heaven,
> where moth and rust do not destroy.
> Matthew 6:20

11   The Mark

Peace—be still! *Peace* when things are going well. *Peace* when everything is going wrong. Peace is the sign of a heart filled with faith. It is the mark I give that tells everyone you are Mine.

Seek peace and pursue it.
Psalm 34:14

12 On the Rock

When you hear My words and do what I say, you are like a house built on a rock. No storm can move you. But when you hear and do not obey, the storm will wash away your kingdom like a castle made of sand.

Whoever hears these words of Mine and does them, will be like a wise man who built his house on rock.
Matthew 7:24 NLV

13 From My Heart

Yes, the mountain before you is high. The path is steep and will be hard to climb. But your desires have all come straight from My heart. Trust Me and move forward without fear. Your power to help others will be nothing short of a miracle.

If you have faith and do not doubt. . .
Matthew 21:21

14 What Needs to Change

Yes, I know. So many things are happening right now. And so much of it is hard to understand. But those things are not really what needs to change. What needs to change is your heart.

Create in me a clean heart, O God.
Psalm 51:10 ESV

15 Awake!

I have a wonderful plan for you—a plan more amazing than anything you could ever hope or dream. When you lay down your goals and begin to search for Me, all your dreams will come true.

Everything else is worthless when compared with the infinite value of knowing Christ Jesus my Lord.
Philippians 3:8 NLT

16 Seek Me First

Trust Me. Put your hand in Mine, and walk with Me today. Seek Me first—before the worries and cares of this busy day have a chance to rush in and drown out the gentle whisper of My love.

O God, You are my God;
Early will I seek You.
Psalm 63:1 NKJV

17 Say the Name

My name is power. It is the name above every name—the name that causes every knee in heaven and earth to bow—every evil to go away, every darkness to burst into heavenly light. My name is *Jesus*.

> At the name of Jesus every knee should bow,
> in heaven and on earth and under the earth.
> Philippians 2:10–11

18 Wait

Do you want to serve Me? Then you must learn to rest and wait. Set down all of your busy fussing and rushing about. Come and sit at My feet. Oh, the miracles I could do if you only learned to wait.

> He went up on a mountainside by himself to pray.
> Matthew 14:23

19 Success

Do you want to be a success? Then you must do what I say. The path of obedience leads to the throne of God. The treasure your heart longs for so very much lies at the end of that amazing road.

Humble yourselves before the Lord,
and he will lift you up.
James 4:10

20 Miracles Again

Wait patiently for Me. Listen carefully for My voice. When you have heard Me, do what I say *no matter what*.

Because the people did not have any faith,
Jesus did not work many miracles there.
Matthew 13:58 CEV

21 ## As I See

Oh, My precious little one, how I long to bless you. Come. Sit with Me. Let Me fill your heart with joy! Close your eyes and see as I see. I love you. I will take care of you. I am your shelter from the storm.

May God be gracious to us and bless us and make his face to shine upon us.
Psalm 67:1 ESV

22 Your Red Sea

Go forward without fear. Do not worry about the Red Sea that lies ahead. When you get there, the waters will part. And you will walk across on dry ground to freedom and your promised land.

All that night the LORD drove the sea back
with a strong east wind and turned it into dry land.
Exodus 14:21

23 Cling to Me

Come. Put your hand in Mine. Let My life flow into yours. I know you are tired. It is time to rest. Put down your burdens. Let Me wash you with waves of joy. I love you. I will take care of you. *Rest.*

He makes me lie down in green pastures, he leads
me beside quiet waters, he restores my soul.
Psalm 23:2–3

24 **The Next Step**

When you know what I want you to do—do it without fear. When you are not really sure, trust Me and take the next step. Don't worry or panic. Just do the job that's right in front of you *and wait*.

The LORD is my light and my salvation—
so why should I be afraid?
Psalm 27:1 NLT

25   Friend of God

You are My friend. And I am yours. Yes, I created the heavens and the earth and everything in them. But they are nothing compared to how much I love you and long to be with you.

Abraham put his trust in God and he became right with God. He was called the friend of God.
James 2:23 NLV

26   Do Not Rush

Why are you in such a hurry? Slow down. Wait for Me. Don't let the little things knock you off of your feet. Little things are *little things*. Leave them to Me—or they will become big things.

Wait for the LORD, my soul waits, and in his word I put my hope.
Psalm 130:5

27 You Are Forgiven

The clouds will part. The sky will become clear.
I am holding you here in My arms. Forget about
the past. The past is gone. Today is a new day.
You are forgiven. Now go and sin no more.

> The eternal God is your refuge,
> and his everlasting arms are under you.
> Deuteronomy 33:27 NLT

28 My Table

Your time of struggle has not been for nothing.
I have set a table before you. It is filled with
wonderful, beautiful, amazing things. So take
what you will. Your cup is full. We will be
together *forever*.

> Goodness and mercy shall follow me
> all the days of my life.
> Psalm 23:6 NKJV

29 Your Joy

You can never go beyond My love and care.
So leave everything to Me. Nothing is impossible.
You cannot see tomorrow. But I can. And I am
working all things together for your good.

Before I say a word, you already know it.
You are all around me.
Psalm 139:4

30 Shine Like the Sun

Take joy with you wherever you go. You have
been blessed. Now you must bless others. Be a ray
of sunshine for each person you meet. Let your
love go around the world—one heart at a time.

Love one another as I have loved you.
John 15:12 ESV

1   Attack Fear

Fear not! My Word is sharper than any two-edged sword. When fear tries to pounce on you, don't back down. Stand your ground—attack! Speak My words of life, and the devil will go away.

For God has not given us a spirit of fear,
but of power and of love and of a sound mind.
2 Timothy 1:7 NKJV

2   Brave and Happy

Is the path ahead slippery and steep? Face it with a brave and happy heart. You don't need to know what will happen tomorrow. All is well. Faith is the heavenly boat that will carry you safely to shore.

God gives what is promised
to the one who keeps on looking for Him.
Hebrews 11:6 NLV

Filled

3

Is your tummy empty? Have something to eat! Is you *heart* empty, sad, lost, or confused? Blessed are those who hunger and thirst to spend this beautiful day with Me—for they will be filled.

> Blessed are those who hunger and thirst
> for righteousness, for they will be filled.
>
> Matthew 5:6

4   I Am Your Friend

I am your friend. Think about it—*your very best friend*! Ready to help. Ready to heal. Ready to give. Mighty to save. More than all you could hope or dream. I am God—I am your friend!

Do not throw away your confidence;
it will be richly rewarded.
Hebrews 10:35

5   I Am Strong

I am with you. Nothing in this world can stop My will from coming to pass. Yes, the storm is raging. And the waves are wild and high. But I am your captain. I will steer your little boat safely to shore.

> I trust you, knowing that you will save me.
> Psalm 25:21 CEV

6   You Will Receive

I will *always* make sure you have everything you need to live and be happy. So trust Me. Take Me at My word. Bury your fears and doubts once and for all. *Ask, and you will receive.*

> Ask, and it will be given to you; seek, and you will find; knock, and it will be opened to you.
> Matthew 7:7 ESV

7   Courage Rewarded

Help, peace, and joy are here. Your courage will be rewarded. Keep on praying. Soon you will see why everything happened as it did. Success will never make you happy. Happiness comes only from Me.

> The Lord disciplines the one he loves.
> Hebrews 12:6 ESV

8   The Secret

I am leading you. As you learn to trust Me more and more, I will begin to show you exactly what I want you to do. So make My goals your goals. Make My dreams your dreams. When you do, those dreams will come true.

> I will instruct you and teach you
> in the way you should go.
> Psalm 32:8 ESV

9   Why Doubt Me?

Joy is like laughter. Let it out, and soon everyone else is laughing as well. So rejoice! Let your heart be filled with joy! Why do you doubt Me? I am your friend. I will always be here at your side.

I will sing to the Lord,
for he has been good to me.
Psalm 13:6

10   Expect Another

I love you. I will take care of you. I am watching over everything you do. So expect a miracle. Then expect another! Every day can be a miracle day when I am welcomed into your happy heart.

What is impossible with man
is possible with God.
Luke 18:27 ESV

11 My Angels

I love you. I will take care of you. You are Mine. You are a child of the King of kings. All heaven's angels stand ready to help and protect you. They are simply waiting for My command.

> He will order his angels
> to protect you wherever you go.
> Psalm 91:11 NLT

12 Expect Good Things

Do you trust Me enough to expect good things? It's easy to sit around and say that nothing good will ever happen. Why? It doesn't take any faith. But without faith *it is impossible to please God.*

> A man cannot please God unless he has faith.
> Hebrews 11:6 NLV

13   Saved

When you pull a drowning man out of the water, what do you do? Throw him back in somewhere deeper? Find a waterfall and toss him over? Of course not! You dry him off and put his feet on solid ground. Why would I do any less for you?

If you confess with your mouth that Jesus is Lord
and believe in your heart that God raised him
from the dead, you will be saved.
Romans 10:9 ESV

14 True Success

Rejoice! I am watching over every part of this beautiful, new day. You are not too young. You will never be too old. You are Mine, and we are eternal—alive and filled with life *forever*!

God, I look to you for help.
I trust in you.
Psalm 141:8

15 Songs on the Way

Some days are dark and lonely. That's nothing to get upset about. It happens to everyone. Paul and Silas were locked in a prison cell. What did they do? They sang Me beautiful songs of praise!

Let everything that has breath praise the LORD.
Psalm 150:6

16 A Safe Place

Trust Me. Know My power. Let Me make your heart My home. Love and laugh. I am watching over you. I am a strong tower. A safe place—an everlasting shelter from each and every storm.

The name of the LORD is a strong tower;
the righteous man runs into it and is safe.
Proverbs 18:10 ESV

17 Peace—Be Still

Peace. Be still! Let your heart be filled with joy. I have so much to teach you. But you cannot learn if your heart is not at rest. So come. Let Me lead you beside still waters. I can make *everything* new.

> He makes me lie down in green pastures.
> He leads me beside still waters. He restores my soul.
> Psalm 23:2–3 ESV

18 Walk Humbly

Trust Me. Give Me your heart. Let Me make everything new. Don't worry about what people will think. Don't worry about what people will say. Just open your heart and welcome Me in.

> This is what he requires of you: to do what is right, to love mercy, and to walk humbly with your God.
> Micah 6:8 NLT

19 Marvelous Miracles

I am with you. Follow Me and do not be afraid. Marvelous things are about to happen. Remember, miracles are what I do naturally. Nothing is ever too big or too difficult for Me.

You stretched out your mighty arm and made the sky and the earth. You can do anything.
Jeremiah 32:17 ESV

20 Simple Things

Oh, My beautiful little one, the things of this world are not for you. Love the simple things. A simple life brings joy and peace. Do what I've asked you to do, and leave the rest to Me.

Do everything as I say, and all will be well.
Jeremiah 7:23 NLT

21   **The Way of Praise**

Did your sunny day become rainy and gray?
Then you must learn to walk the way of praise.
When trouble comes, think of everything you
have to be thankful for. Then praise, praise, praise!

Sing to the Lord a new song.
Sing his praises in the assembly of the faithful.
Psalm 149:1 NLT

22 Greater Works

Greater Works! The blind can see. The lame can walk. The sick are healed. The world can hear the good news about My Son. Yes, you can ask for anything in My name—anything—*and I will do it*!

Whoever believes in me will also do the works that
I do; and greater works than these will he do,
because I am going to the Father.
John 14:12 ESV

23 The Missing Peace

I have a gift for you—a gift that no one can ever take away. That gift is *My peace*. Are you worried or afraid? You must have misplaced it. Stop everything and search *for Me* until you get it back.

The peace of God, which surpasses
all understanding, will guard your hearts.
Philippians 4:7 NKJV

24   Close to Me

Do you need to know which way to go? Then stay close to Me. I am the way, the truth, and the life. The secret to a powerful, peaceful, clean, pure heart is simply to stay very, very close to Me.

I am the way and the truth and the life.
John 14:6

25 Wonderful Life

I am your friend. The Lord of your life! This good day and everything in it are safe in the palm of My hand. I will lead you. I will guide your every step. Your life is My life—and that life is *wonderful*!

> With long life will I satisfy him
> and show him my salvation.
> Psalm 91

26 Forgive and Forget

Forget the past. The past is gone! Fill this good day with love and laughter. Forgive *everything* and treat *everyone* just like you would treat Me.

> Lord, how many times shall I forgive my brother
> when he sins against me?
> Matthew 18:21

27 Walk with Me

Oh, My little one, how I love to be with you. If you only knew the joy that fills My heart when we are together! Come, walk with Me again today.

Come, let us go up to Zion,
to the LORD our God.
Jeremiah 31:6

28   Jump with Joy

I am your shield. Nothing this world throws at you
can harm you. Yes, you made a few mistakes. You
will make a few more. Your road will have bumps.
But I will teach you to jump over them with joy.

The LORD is my strength and shield.
I trust him with all my heart. He helps me,
and my heart is filled with joy.
Psalm 28:7 NLT

29   Glad and Green

In this world you will have trouble. But rejoice!
The path ahead is filled with sunshine. The trees
are blooming, glad and green. The hills are alive
with the scent of beautiful flowers. For I am God
Almighty—and I have overcome the world!

I have overcome the world.
John 16:33

30   Faith Rewarded

Abraham belived My promise—and had more children than the stars in the sky. Moses believed My promise—and My people saw the Promised Land. Trust Me today—I reward those who seek Me!

> He rewards those who sincerely seek him.
> Hebrews 11:6 NLT

31   A Thankful Heart

Do you want to make Me glad? Give Me the gift of a thankful heart! Leave no stone unturned in your search for new and amazing ways to thank Me for all the good things I have done.

> He fell to the ground at Jesus' feet, thanking him for what he had done.
> Luke 17:16 NLT

1   **Friendship**

I will never leave you. I will never take My love away. There is no power in heaven or earth that could ever make Me stop loving you. Our hearts are one. Our lives are one. You are My friend.

I will never leave you nor forsake you.
Hebrews 13:5 ESV

2 The Harvest

I love to bless you. And I will. But before a seed can be planted, the ground must be made ready. Your heart is like that good ground. Prayer is the tool that makes it ready for a harvest of blessings.

> Still other seed fell on good soil,
> where it produced a crop.
> Matthew 13:8

3 Love or Money

I love when you give. For there are so many people in need. But never think that money is the greatest gift you have to offer. The greatest gift is *love*.

> And now these three remain: faith, hope and love.
> But the greatest of these is love.
> 1 Corinthians 13:13

4   Alive Forever

You are alive with the life that comes from heaven. The wonderful new life I placed in your heart will last *forever*. Now, when you share that new life, the things you say and do will be alive forever, too.

> My sheep hear My voice and I know them.
> They follow Me. I give them life that lasts forever.
> John 10:27–28 NLV

5   In Time of Need

I am your healer. Your joy. Your Lord. Call My name and I will be there. I have been here all the time. Silently watching. Silently protecting. Your time of need is My time to appear.

> Call to Me, and I will answer you,
> and show you great and mighty things.
> Jeremiah 33:3 NKJV

6 Quiet Times

Come. Rest with Me. If the Son of God needed quiet times with the Father, then surely you must need them, too.

Shut your door, pray to your Father
who is in the secret place; and your Father
who sees in secret will reward you openly.
Matthew 6:6 NKJV

7   All Is Well

Why are you worried? All is well. You don't *ever* have to be afraid. Oh, My little one, trust Me! Say these words until you know them by heart: "I love you. I will take care of you. *All is well.*"

God, I look to you for help. I trust in you.
Psalm 141:8

8   Empty Yourself

Stop trying to save yourself. Ask Me for help! Take what I give, and then ask for more. Don't hold back. Trust Me completely. Empty yourself. I will fill you—again and again and again.

If anyone is thirsty,
let him come to me and drink.
John 7:37

9 Home

Come. Talk to Me. Make My heart your home.
My paths are straight. My way is safe and sure.
There is a treasure waiting for you. Find it, and
you will live forever!

Show me your ways, O LORD,
teach me your paths; guide me in your truth.
Psalm 25:4–5

10 My Little Sheep

You are My little sheep. I am your shepherd.
Stay close to Me, and all will be well. Nothing
can hurt you while you are by My side.

The Lord is my shepherd; I will have everything I need.
He lets me rest in fields of green grass.
He leads me beside the quiet waters.
He makes me strong again.
Psalm 23:1–3 NLT

11 You Are Mine

Trust Me. Believe Me! You are Mine. You don't ever have to be afraid. I made the heavens and the earth. I hung the stars in the sky. Take My hand. I will lead you out of the darkness and into the light.

> I have kept watch over those You gave Me.
> Not one of them has been lost.
> John 17:12 NLV

12 This Is the Time

Remember, I hear and answer every prayer. Has something suddenly gone wrong? Have things turned dark and gray? Don't give up and run away. This is not the time to quit. *This is the time to pray!*

> By the grace of God I am what I am,
> and His grace toward me was not in vain.
> 1 Corinthians 15:10 NKJV

Perfect

Don't worry about what people think. Don't worry about what people say. You don't have to be *anyone* but you. I love you. *I created you.* You are perfect—just the way you are.

I praise you because of the wonderful way
you created me. Everything you do is marvelous!
Psalm 139:14 CEV

14 The Greatest Gift

Life is a gift—a gift from heaven. It is the greatest gift I have to give—a free gift for *anyone* who is brave enough to take it! So reach out. Open your heart. Let Me fill it with treasure from heaven.

It is no longer I who live,
but Christ who lives in me.
Galatians 2:20 ESV

15   Follow Me

I will guide you in everything you do. You are not being punished for the mistakes of the past. But you must follow Me and do as I say. I have a plan for you. I will use you. *But you must follow Me.*

This happened so the power of God
could be seen in him.
John 9:3 NLT

16   Tired Work

Tired work is never good work. It always has to be done again. If you keep on forcing it, something will break! So stop and rest. *Stop right now.* Let Me take your frazzled nerves and give them peace.

I am leaving you with a gift—
peace of mind and heart.
John 14:27 NLT

17   Nature Sings

Come to Me. Come out and play. All of creation is waiting here for you! My sun is shining. My birds are singing. Let them fill your heart with joy!

The heavens declare the glory of God;
the skies proclaim the work of his hands.
Psalm 19:1

18   Along the Way

Two children went on a trip. One skipped happily from each flower to the next, enjoying the sights along the way. The other kicked and screamed at every turn. Both went to the same places. Both saw the same things. But only one truly followed Me.

I delight to do Your will, O my God.
Psalm 40:8 NKJV

19 My Temple

You are My temple—a living, breathing offering of thanksgiving and praise. Bow down before Me. Let Me fill you with My glory. My power to give is only limited by your willingness to receive.

And they spent all of their time
in the Temple, praising God.
Luke 24:53 NLT

20 Spread Your Wings

You have given Me your heart. And I have given your heart wings—wings that will carry you all the way to heaven. So forget the past. You are no longer a caterpillar. You are a beautiful butterfly. Spread your wings and learn to fly.

The old life is gone; a new life has begun!
2 Corinthians 5:17 NKJV

21 **Sing Again**

Behold—I make all things new! Every good gift you have was sent to break the chains that tie your heart to this weary world. Let My blessings heal your broken heart so you can sing again.

I will sing a new song to you, O God.
Psalm 144:9

22 Rays of Sunshine

Your pains and trials are a gift. They are the keys that can unlock the chains of a broken heart. So share what you know with someone in need. It will fill their gray day with rays of sunshine.

You have kept my feet from falling,
so I may walk with God in the light of life.
Psalm 56:13 NLV

23 Look Up!

You are climbing a mountain. Don't let every little stone and stumble put you out of sorts. The view from the top will be absolutely amazing. So remember, don't look down—look up!

If we are faithful to the end,
trusting God just as firmly as when we first believed,
we will share in all that belongs to Christ.
Hebrews 3:14 NLT

24 Keep On Climbing

I love you. I am your *heavenly Father*. I will do the very best for you—each and every time. So trust Me with everything. And keep on climbing. *All things are possible* when your heart belongs to Me.

The LORD is my rock
and my fortress and my deliverer;
My God, my strength, in whom I will trust.
Psalm 18:2 NKJV

25   Side by Side

If you seek Me, you will find Me. No one ever asked for My help without success. Yes, My way is narrow. But there is plenty of room for both of us to walk side by side. Call out My name. I will be there.

You will seek me and find me
when you seek me with all your heart.
Jeremiah 29:13

26   Fear Not

In this world you will have trouble. But don't let that bother you. Let your heart be filled with joy! I am watching over everything in your life. All things are working together *for your good*.

Fear not, for I have redeemed you;
I have called you by name, you are mine.
Isaiah 43:1 ESV

27 Untangled

Trust Me. Give Me your tangled, mixed-up life, and let Me make it new. Yes, it will take time. And it may even hurt a little. But I love you. And I will make everything clear and true.

In quietness and trust is your strength
Isaiah 30:15 NLT

28 Longing to Help

A heart that longs to help is like a gift sent from heaven. It can turn darkness into light, sadness into joy, hopelessness into healing, a bitter end into a sweet new beginning.

My eyes will look with favor
on the faithful in the land.
Psalm 101:6 NLV

29 In My Name

Oh, My little one, reach out your tiny hand. Put it in Mine. Squeeze tight and say My name. Jesus! Jesus! Strength and healing. Power and might. Everything you will ever need is in My name!

God. . .gave him the name that is
above every name.
Philippians 2:9

30 Give, Give, Give

Give and keep on giving. Everything I have is yours. So open your heart. Give hope. Give peace. Give kindness. Give love. Reach out your hand and give someone the gift of heaven.

A generous man will himself be blessed.
Proverbs 22:9

31 Closer to Me

Do you want to help others? Then you must come closer and closer to Me. Your prayers are the wood that will keep the fire burning. Our time together is the spark that will fan it into flame.

This kind can come out only by prayer.
Mark 9:29

1 Rich Indeed

I will never leave you. I will never take My love away. Everything I have is yours. My love will never fail you. My strength will always be there. My patience has no end. You are rich indeed!

Be content with what you have, for he has said,
"I will never leave you nor forsake you."
Hebrews 13:5 ESV

2   I Will Provide

I am God. I will always give you everything you need. Fill your heart with a beautiful garden of faith and trust. Water it with a happy, thankful heart, and watch what I will do.

Abraham called the name of that place,
"The Lord will provide."
Genesis 22:14 ESV

3   More of Heaven

Why are you worried? Why are you afraid? Look up! Lift your eyes to heaven. Walk with Me. Talk to Me. Run into My arms. Let Me make your heart My *forever* home.

I remember your wonderful deeds of long ago.
They are constantly in my thoughts.
Psalm 77:11–12 NLT

4

Set It Down

Drop your burdens. Drop them all! Lay your worries and fears at My feet, *and leave them there.* Stop trying to carry them. They are much too heavy. Trust Me, and let your happy heart sing.

Cast your cares on the LORD and he will sustain you; he will never let the righteous fall.
Psalm 55:22

5   Growing Up

Blooming and growing are the laws of heaven.
So stretch out your hands. Stretch out your heart.
Turn and open your face to the sun. Let My light
and My warmth draw you closer to heaven.

Your righteousness reaches to the skies, O God.
Psalm 71:19

6   Your Loved Ones

Your loved ones are safe and secure in My arms.
But, oh, how they need your kindness and prayers.

Dear friends, let us continue
to love one another, for love comes from God.
Anyone who loves is a child of God.
1 John 4:7 NLT

7   My Arms

My arms are strong and mighty. They will protect
you from every storm. They are your help in times
of trouble. They are your hiding place when you
are afraid. They are holding you right now.

The eternal God is your refuge,
and his everlasting arms are under you.
Deuteronomy 33:27 NLT

8   Clogged

Has your well run dry? Something is clogging
the pipe! Give freely with a happy heart, and all
of heaven's blessing will begin to flow again.

Give, and it will be given to you.
Luke 6:38

9 First Things First

We need to work on *your* garden first. So let's get to it! Pull up the weeds. Turn over the soil. Plant the seeds. Prune the vines! When *your ground* is ready, we can begin to work on others.

I am the vine; you are the branches. If a man remains in me and I in him, he will bear much fruit.
John 15:5–7

10 God and Money

Do you want every good and perfect gift I have to give? Do you want every good thing the world has to offer as well? Then you are trying to serve both God and money.

You cannot serve both God and money.
Matthew 6:24

11 My Pleasure

Our lives are one—yours and Mine. Every good thing I have flows freely from My heart to yours. I am the vine. You are the branches. Fear not! It is My good pleasure to give you the kingdom.

Fear not, little flock, for it is your Father's good pleasure to give you the kingdom.
Luke 12:32 ESV

12   Money?

Why are you worried about something as worthless as money? If your heart's desire is to know Me and do My will, then your life, and the lives of *everyone* around you, will be filled with heavenly light.

Seek first the kingdom of God and his righteousness, and all these things will be added to you.
Matthew 6:33 ESV

13   No Other Name

There is no other name in heaven or on earth that has the power to save—no other name that can turn darkness into light, sadness into joy, even death into life—but the wonderful name of Jesus.

There is no other name under heaven given to men by which we must be saved.
Acts 4:12

14   Look for the Path

Oh, My precious little one, *trust Me*. Look for the path that will lead you to My side. Walk it with courage, faith, and joy. It will lead you to heaven.

Lord, I believe;
help my unbelief!
Mark 9:24 NKJV

15 Quiet Strength

This world sees strength as noise and action. But I see strength as quietness and rest. So when you feel like you've run out of gas, don't get out and push—rest and fill up with power from *heaven*.

The LORD gives strength to his people;
the LORD blesses his people with peace.
Psalm 29:11

16 Right on Time

There is no need to hurry. I won't be late. We have all the time in heaven and earth. So peace, be still! Your dreams will come true. Faith is the rain that will make them bloom—right on time.

The fruit of righteousness will be peace.
Isaiah 32:17

17 This Is the Way

You are on the right path. *This is the way.* I know you can't see where we are going. I know you don't always know what to do. Don't be afraid. Just take the next step. I am leading you. This *is* the way.

Show me your ways, O Lord,
teach me your paths.
Psalm 25:4

18 Live There

Oh, My little one, I have so many good things for you. But you must draw near if you want to find them. My Secret Place is filled with treasure. Visitors never see it. But those who *live there* find it all.

He who dwells in the secret place of the Most High
Shall abide under the shadow of the Almighty.
Psalm 91:1 NKJV

19   Filled with Joy

The lessons I give are a gift. Open them gladly, and your heart will be filled with joy. Search for them each day like hidden treasure. Let them fill your heart and home with laughter and love.

These things I have spoken to you, that my joy may
be in you, and that your joy may be full.
John 15:11 ESV

20   Wait and See

God is good. All is well. You are safe here in My arms. Trust Me. Rest. Don't be afraid. I will help. Just wait and see!

Taste and see that the LORD is good;
blessed is the man who takes refuge in him.
Psalm 34:8

21 If You've Seen Me

Have you seen Me? Do you know who I am?
Here is a clue—I am loving. Giving. Filled with
kindness. Slow to anger. Quick to forgive. Faithful.
Merciful. Always available. *I am Jesus.* And if you
have seen Me—you have seen God.

Anyone who has seen me
has seen the Father.
John 14:9

22 Sing!

Sing to Me with a glad and happy heart. Sing a beautiful, new song. Worship is a gift. It fills My heart with joy. So sing to Me with songs of worship and praise!

It is good to sing praises to our God.
For it is pleasing and praise is right.
Psalm 147:1 NLV

23 Turn to Me

Turn your heart to Me, and I will come near. There is no need to beg. You don't ever have to make a deal. You don't need to say a single word. Just open your heart, and I will be there.

Draw near to God,
and he will draw near to you.
James 4:8 ESV

24   Learn and Live

Every good teacher will lead you back to Me. Always be thankful for a teacher like that. But remember—never, ever follow a teacher who tries to lead you to anyone or anything else.

Lord, to whom shall we go?
You have the words of eternal life.
John 6:68

25 Come and Stay

Have you been running in crazy circles? Come to Me and rest. But when you come—stop—and stay long enough to let Me fill you with My peace.

Come to me. . .and I will give you rest.
Matthew 11:28 ESV

26 A Welcome Guest

Do your best to help each person you meet. Treat everyone as if you were a servant—and they were a welcome guest—in My Father's house. Remember, whatever you do for them, you also do for Me.

Serve one another in love.
Galatians 5:13

27 All Heaven Waits

My power to save has no limits. But I will never force myself on anyone. Oh, how often I have longed to help. And how painful it has been to wait for that broken heart to call out My name.

The Lord's hand is not so short that it cannot save, and His ear is not closed that it cannot hear.
Isaiah 59:1 NLV

28 The Way of Sadness

Oh, My little one, do not be afraid to share your heart with another. The way of sadness is not an easy path to walk. But, oh, the joy you will bring if you dare to walk it with your friend.

His compassions never fail. They are new every morning; great is your faithfulness.
Lamentations 3:22–23

29 My Touch

My touch will bring healing. My touch will bring strength. My touch will bring courage, wisdom, and power. So quiet your heart. Wait and be still. I will reach out My hand—but you must *be still*.

Then he touched their eyes and said,
"According to your faith will it be done to you";
and their sight was restored.
Matthew 9:29–30

30 Wisdom

Do you need wisdom? All you have to do is ask. I have more than enough for today. I will have more than enough for tomorrow. So trust Me. Take what you need. Use it up. Then ask for more.

If you do not have wisdom, ask God for it.
He is always ready to give.
James 1:5 NLV

1   Milk and Honey

I will never leave you. I will always take care of you. You don't ever have to be afraid. I fed My children with food from heaven. I parted the Red Sea. I led My children through the wilderness and into a land flowing with milk and honey. And I will do the same for you.

I will lead you to a land
flowing with milk and honey.
Exodus 3:17 NLT

2 The Humble

What a joy it is to lead you when you trust Me with all of your heart. You will never know the pain that comes from arguing, complaining, and trying to go your own way.

Seek the LORD, all who are humble,
and follow his commands.
Zephaniah 2:3 NLT

3 Be Still and Know

Be still and know that I am God. When your heart and mind are quiet, I can work miracles. For a quiet heart is a heart that trusts Me. And a heart that trusts Me can do amazing things.

The fruit of righteousness will be peace.
Isaiah 32:17

The Light of Life

4

When you let My Spirit guide you, your life will be filled with heavenly light. So don't be surprised if your old ways start to seem a little odd. Everything looks different when you see it in heaven's light.

He will see the light of life
and be satisfied.
Isaiah 53:11

5 Every Step

I love you. I will take care of you. I will never, ever make a mistake. Nothing I do will be an accident. I am watching over you. And I will bless you— each and every step of the way.

My help comes from the LORD,
the Maker of heaven and earth.
Psalm 121:2

6 Hand in Hand

Trust Me. Hang on to Me. Put your little hand in Mine. All is well. Your faith will be rewarded. Why would I fail you? How could I fail you? Nothing is too big or too difficult for Me.

The LORD your God goes with you;
he will never leave you nor forsake you.
Deuteronomy 31:6

7   Weakness

When you are weak, I am strong. So be happy! Let your heart be filled with joy. My power works best in the hands of weak people. So trust Me. I am with you. Lean on My love and know all is well.

My grace is sufficient for you,
for my power is made perfect in weakness.
2 Corinthians 12:9 ESV

8   The Darkest Places

Are fear and doubt creeping into your heart? Shut them out! Think about My love. Talk to Me! Soon joy will flow into the darkest places, and your heart will be filled with heavenly light.

Even the darkness is not dark to you;
the night is bright as the day.
Psalm 139:12 ESV

9 My Little Sheep

You are My beautiful little sheep. I am your shepherd. I will show you the way to go. Don't ever be afraid to ask Me for help. Every word you pray draws My heart closer and closer to you.

He makes me lie down in green pastures.
He leads me beside still waters. He restores my soul.
Psalm 23:1–3 ESV

10 More Work

I am your helper. Keep on walking. A wonderful blessing is waiting at the end of this road. There is more work ahead. So do it with joy. I am with you. I am leading you. Everything will be alright.

If you are willing and obedient,
you will eat the best from the land.
Isaiah 1:19

11 No Ruffled Feathers

Peace. Be still! Don't let anyone or anything ruffle your feathers. Breathe in My stillness like the cool air on a golden fall morning. Let it blow away the cares of this noisy, crazy, hurried world.

The LORD will hear when I call to him.
Psalm 4:3

12 Out of the Darkness

Have you wandered down the path of fear and doubt? The first step out of the darkness is praise! So steady your heart. Find a reason to thank Me. Ask Me for help. Then give Me praise!

I prayed to the LORD, and he answered me.
He freed me from all my fears.
Psalm 34:4 NLT

13 The Artist

I am the Artist. You are the masterwork My love is creating. When I find a cracked stone, I toss it aside. But when I find a rare treasure like you, I mold it and make it into a beautiful work of art.

We are the clay, you are the potter;
we are all the work of your hand.
Isaiah 64:8

14   The Lamb of God

I am Jesus—the Lamb of God. Lay your sins at the foot of the cross. Let My blood wash them as white as snow. Forget the past. The past is gone. You have been forgiven. *You are free!*

Look! The Lamb of God
who takes away the sin of the world!
John 1:29 NLT

15 My Very Best

Come. Make your home with Me. Every gift heaven holds is waiting for you there. You are not a poor beggar. You are a child of the King. Let Me give My very best to you.

Seek first the kingdom of God and his righteousness, and all these things will be added to you.
Matthew 6:33 ESV

16 Set Them Free

Worry, fear, and doubt are like a prison. When you give in to their lies, you lock My blessings away in the dark. Courage and faith are the keys that will open the door and set them free.

The doors of the jail broke open, and all the prisoners were freed.
Acts 16:26 NCV

17 Faith That Sees

Where are you looking? What do you see? Is your heart troubled? It is time to turn your back on the dirt and darkness of this broken world and turn your eyes on the beauty and joy found only in Me.

The eye is the lamp of the body. If your eyes are good, your whole body will be full of light.
Matthew 6:22

18 A Broken Heart

Oh, My little one, I know what it means to have a broken heart. Don't waste your life trying to be famous. The wealthy and powerful did not build My kingdom. They tossed Me aside and ran away.

Everyone deserted him and fled.
Mark 14:50

19   When I Answer

I hear everyone who quiets their heart to pray.
But, oh, how few people there are who are quiet
enough on the inside to hear Me when I answer.

I pray to you, God, because you will help me.
Listen and answer my prayer!
Psalm 17:6 CEV

20   Bumps in the Road

When you do My will with gladness and joy, the
bumps in the road will not topple your cart. Did
you hit a few potholes? Leave those wobbly wheels
to Me.

Show me what you want me to do,
and let your gentle Spirit lead me in the right path.
Psalm 143:10 CEV

21   At the Door

Is your heart open to Me? Behold—I stand at the door of your heart and knock! If you hear My voice and open your heart to Me, I will come in. Then we will enjoy being together.

Behold, I stand at the door and knock. If anyone hears my voice and opens the door, I will come in.
Revelation 3:20 ESV

22 House Building

I am building a beautiful house. Its foundation—
the part that holds everything else up—has been
built with mighty blocks of unshakable faith. Now
fill up its rooms with a thankful, quiet, happy heart.

We will come to him
and make our home with him.
John 14:23

23 Like Abraham

You must learn to trust Me all the way to the end.
Like Abraham, keep on trusting even when the
road ahead disappears into the mist. Ignore what
you see—or what you cannot see—and trust in Me.

The just shall live by faith.
Romans 1:17 NKJV

24 Salt of the Earth

You are the salt of the earth. When you are at your freshest and best, this world can be a delicious place. But if that salt loses its flavor—oh, how tasteless everything and everyone becomes. Stay close to Me, and help flavor the world with My love.

You are the salt of the earth. But if the salt loses its saltiness, how can it be made salty again?
Matthew 5:13

25 Waiting and Working

There are no empty hours in the kingdom of heaven. Waiting isn't easy. In some ways, it's harder than work. But the only way to wait *without worry* on the outside is to trust Me completely *on the inside*.

Better a patient man than a warrior, a man who controls his temper than one who takes a city.
Proverbs 16:32

26 I Don't Know the Man

When my enemies doubt Me, I never wonder why. When those who mock Me refuse to trust Me, it comes as no surprise. But when My children, who know and love Me, are afraid to call My name—that pain is more than My heart can bear.

He denied it again, with an oath:
"I don't know the man!"
Matthew 26:72

27   Days of Winning

You are not perfect. And yes, you have made a few mistakes. But I am not looking at that. I know you are fighting a hard battle. So be happy! You have won—for I am looking *at your heart.*

He will save my soul in peace
from those who make war against me.
Psalm 55:18 NLV

28   A Wonderful Surprise

Come. Bow down before Me. Open up your heart. Close your eyes. No more peeking! Yes, it's true— I have a wonderful surprise waiting just for you.

Let the little children come to me.
Luke 18:16

Success

Never measure your success by the amount of money you have gained. This is not the way for you. Success is measured by your desire to do My will—and the love you have for your friends.

It is easier for a camel to go through
the eye of a needle than for a rich man
to enter the kingdom of God.
Matthew 19:24

30 A Harvest Lesson

You cannot pick apples before you plant a tree. You cannot be a farmer if you won't put a seed in the ground. But, oh, My child—if you can learn to wait—*you will see your dreams come true.*

Those who wait on the LORD
shall renew their strength.
Isaiah 40:31 NKJV

31 My Voice

Read My Word. Hide it in your heart. The Word is My voice—the voice of heaven. My Word will lead you. It is the voice of wisdom. The voice of healing. The voice of your friend.

Your word is a lamp to guide my feet
and a light for my path.
Psalm 119:105 NLT

November

1   Prayers of Joy

Your prayers are a like beautiful fragrance. They rise up from a heart of faith and spread their sweet perfume all over heaven, swirling beneath wings of joy that bring My blessings to earth.

Let my prayer be set before You as incense,
The lifting up of my hands as the evening sacrifice.
Psalm 141:2 NKJV

2 Spend It All

Give and keep on giving. Bring Me an empty container, and let Me fill it up. Take what you need, and then *spend all the rest*. Find an empty heart and fill it to the top with gladness and joy.

> Give, and it will be given to you.
> You will have more than enough.
> Luke 6:38 NLV

3 No End

There is no end to My power—no end to the wonderful, incredible things I can do. So trust Me. Don't hold Me back! Have a big faith. Expect big things, and you will get big things!

> You can ask for anything in my name, and I will do it, so that the Son can bring glory to the Father.
> John 14:13 NLT

4

I Am with You

I am with you. I am right here beside you. I will never leave you or take My love away. Reach out. Take My hand. Let Me fill your heart with joy. I am with you *always*.

In Your presence is fullness of joy.
Psalm 16:11 NKJV

5 Coming Soon

I am coming soon—as soon as all those who hear My name will bow their hearts and let Me use them to tell someone else the Good News.

And now, little children, abide in Him, that when He appears, we may have confidence and not be ashamed before Him at His coming.
1 John 2:28 NKJV

6 With Power

You are never too weak. You are never too small. You are never too young or too old or too tired. Just call out My name, and I will move. But watch out! When I move, I move with power!

May your hope grow stronger by the power of the Holy Spirit.
Romans 15:13 NLV

7 The Pipeline

Yes, you are small. But you are mighty. You are the pipeline that carries My love to this world. So keep the pipe clean. And watch out for clogs. My love and My power are coming through!

> By God's power
> we will live with him to serve you.
> 2 Corinthians 13:4

8 A Clean Slate

Forget the past. The past is gone! Wipe the slate clean, and start over again. Erase your mistakes and failures. Erase the memory of anything anyone did to hurt you. *Forget it all* and begin again.

> I forget everything that is behind me
> and look forward to that which is ahead.
> Philippians 3:13 NLV

9   Wonderful Friendship

I am God Almighty—the maker of heaven and earth. I hung the stars in the sky. I spoke, and the sun came alive. I filled every inch of this beautiful world with life. And I am your friend!

"Abraham put his trust in God and he became right with God." He was called the friend of God.
James 2:23 NLV

10   New Power

Don't stop when trouble tries to stand in your way. Don't even slow down. Call out My name. Ask for new power! Charge boldly ahead with courage and strength, and push all trouble aside.

Now all glory to God,
who is able to keep you from falling.
Jude 1:24 NLT

11 The Color of Heaven

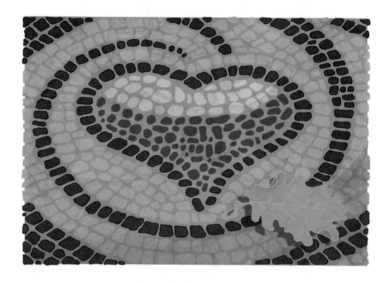

I am watching over every step you take. So relax and leave everything to Me. The color of heaven is a wonderful mosaic laid one stone at a time. I will make sure all things are beautiful in their time.

When he tests me, I will come out as pure as gold.
For I have stayed on God's paths.
Job 23:10–11 NLT

12   The Silent Cry

The wisdom of men, no matter how wise, can do nothing to answer the questions of a life that is lost and alone in the dark. But the silent cry of a broken heart is heard above all the music of heaven.

Anyone who claims to know all the answers
doesn't really know very much.
1 Corinthians 8:2 NLT

13   Come Unto Me

Are you sick? Come to Me for healing. Are you lost? Come to Me to find the way home. Are you lonely? Come to Me, and you will find a friend. Whatever you need—come to Me!

Come unto me. . .and I will give you rest.
Matthew 11:28 KJV

14 Disobedient Hearts

Disobedient hearts make straight paths crooked.
Evil men block the road with jagged stones.
This is not the world My Father's heart created.
But rejoice—for I have overcome the world!

Prepare the way for the LORD.
Isaiah 40:3

15 By My Spirit

My miracles were not just "Once Upon a Time."
They are who I am. And I am the same yesterday,
today, and *forever*! Do you believe this?

> " 'Not by might nor by power,
> but by my Spirit,' says the LORD."
> Zechariah 4:6

16 Togetherness Is Power

When two of you come together to love and help
others, I will be with you in power. Nothing will
be too difficult. Nothing will be impossible. For
I will be there with you.

> Where two or three come together in my name,
> there am I with them.
> Matthew 18:20

17   Quiet Lives

Not to the famous or powerful. Not to the great and mighty. But to the quiet and unseen. To those who serve Me with all of their heart—to *those* ears I whisper, "Well done, good and faithful servant."

Well done,
good and faithful servant!
Matthew 25:21

18   The Glory of God

Have you blessed a lonely heart with kindness? Have you calmed an angry heart with love? Have you lifted a heavy load with your happy heart? Then you have shown others the Glory of God.

Lord, I believe; help my unbelief!
Mark 9:24 NKJV

19   **To the Hills**

Lift up your eyes. Lift them to the hills. Look up!
I am coming. Your help is already on the way!

> I lift up my eyes to the hills—
> where does my help come from?
> My help comes from the LORD,
> the Maker of heaven and earth.
> Psalm 121:1–2

20   **Mysteries**

What will the future hold? Only time will tell.
But one thing is certain. When your heart is
longing to know the mysteries of heaven, the
future will hold more and more of Me.

> No eye has seen, no ear has heard, no mind
> has conceived what God has prepared
> for those who love him.
> 1 Corinthians 2:9

21   Little Lights

When you light a candle, what do you do with it? Do you hide it under the bed? Do you put it where no one can see? No! You set it on a stand. You are like that candle. So stand up! Let everyone see your light—and let them know it comes from Me.

A lamp is placed on a stand,
where it gives light to everyone in the house.
Matthew 5:15 NLT

22 Love That Lasts

The most beautiful words of the world's greatest speaker can fall silently to the ground. No one may hear or be helped by them at all. But *love someone*, and you have created a miracle that will last *forever*.

If I speak in the tongues of men and of angels,
but have not love. . .I gain nothing.
1 Corinthians 13:1–3

23 Take Heart!

The evil one tried to destroy Me. And because you are Mine, he will try to destroy you. But take heart! No power in heaven or earth can stand against Me—and nothing will be able to harm you either.

In this world you will have trouble. But take heart!
I have overcome the world.
John 16:33

24 Something Special

Each new day brings a chance to do something special for Me. Give Me this day as an offering. Your happy heart can be a blessing to everyone. Love others deeply. I will bless you for it.

Above all, love each other deeply,
because love covers over a multitude of sins.
1 Peter 4:8

25 Stand at the Door

Do you know someone who has locked the door to their heart? Don't walk away. Stand at the door, and knock with gentle kindness until they are ready to open the door and welcome Me inside.

Behold, I stand at the door and knock.
Revelation 3:20 NKJV

26 Beautiful

My face was never beautiful. My body was not strong. When people looked at Me, they didn't see a mighty leader. They didn't see anything they wanted at all! Why not? The answer is simple. They were so busy looking at My outside that they could not see My heart.

He had no beauty or majesty
to attract us to him.
Isaiah 53:2

27   The Choice

When you pray, I will answer. But I will never force My answer on you. My way will always be the best way. And to find it, you must follow Me. But the choice to follow will always be up to you.

> Not my will, but yours be done.
> Luke 22:42

28   Change

Do you want to do great things? Do you want to change this weary, broken world? That is a very good thing. And I will help you do it. But before any of that can happen—first, I must change you.

> Since we are living by the Spirit, let us follow
> the Spirit's leading in every part of our lives.
> Galatians 5:25 NLT

29 When Two Agree

When two of you agree in prayer about *anything*, it will be done for you by My Father in heaven. That is My promise. But remember—asking and *believing I will answer* are two very different things.

If two of you on earth agree about anything you ask for, it will be done for you by my Father in heaven.
Matthew 18:19

30 Sanctuary

I am your sanctuary—your hiding place in times of trouble. You can hide from the problems and cares of other people in many different ways. But the only place to hide *from your own troubles* is to stay very close to Me.

You are my hiding place; you protect me from trouble. You surround me with songs of victory.
Psalm 32:7 NLT

1   **Step by Step**

You won't be able to solve every puzzle. Some questions will never be answered on this side of heaven. But don't let that trouble you. Answers or not, I am leading you every step of the way.

> There is so much more I want to tell you,
> but you can't bear it now.
> John 16:12 NLT

2   Holy Ground

Come. Draw near to Me. Take off your shoes. The place where you are standing is holy ground. I am not far away or hard to find. I am God. I am here. I am your friend.

Take off your sandals,
for you are standing on holy ground.
Exodus 3:5 NLT

3   Friend of Sinners

I am with you. I know how you feel. I know you are weak. I know you are trying to do the right thing. I know you have failed. I am the friend of sinners. If you let Me, I will make everything new.

I tell you, her sins—and they are many—
have been forgiven.
Luke 7:47 NLT

4 Man of Sorrows

This world showers its heroes with riches and fame. But it turned its back on the Son of God. When you follow Me, it will turn its back on you, too. Don't be discouraged. Let the sticks and stones fly. You have a treasure this world will never know.

He is despised and rejected by men,
A Man of sorrows and acquainted with grief.
Isaiah 53:3 NKJV

5 A Cheerful Giver

I love a cheerful giver. So let your happy heart give a special gift to everyone you meet. Give love, joy, patience, kindness, forgiveness, prayer, a helping hand—anything you can to bless those you meet.

Love your enemies, bless those who curse you,
do good to those who hate you.
Matthew 5:44 NKJV

Temptation

The enemy tried to get Me to sin. He will do the same to you. Don't let your heart be troubled. When sin tries to pull you away, I will make a way for you to escape—but it's up to you to take it!

When you are tempted,
he will show you a way out.
1 Corinthians 10:13 NLT

7   Bread of Life

When your tummy is hungry, what do you do? You get something to eat. Your heart can get hungry in the very same way. My Word and My will are the food your heart needs to be happy and full.

"My food," said Jesus, "is to do the will of him who sent me and to finish his work."
John 4:34

8   My Kingdom

When they took Me from the cross and put Me in the grave, my followers thought all was lost. But they were wrong. The grave had no power to hold Me. All was not lost. All was found!

Whoever lives and believes in me will never die. Do you believe this?
John 11:26

9   Seekers Rewarded

Do you know someone who is a seeker? What do you think they are seeking? I'll let you in on a secret: they are not really sure. But you know, don't you? Why not help them to find Me today?

> If you search for him with all your heart and soul, you will find him.
> Deuteronomy 4:29 NLT

10   Silence

Sometimes I will speak. Other times, I am silent. Either way—trust Me. Sometimes I must be silent for a very long time. That doesn't mean I don't love you. I am just trying to draw you closer to My side.

> Speak, LORD, for your servant is listening.
> 1 Samuel 3:9

11   My Sunrise Gift

This good new day is a gift. It is My sunrise gift to you. Unwrap it with joy. Live simply, and do the little things well. My love can make anything new. So expect good things. Expect *great* things!

The hope of the righteous brings joy.
Proverbs 10:28 ESV

12 Carefree

Love and fear cannot live in the same house. Evil is powerful. And fear is one of its favorite weapons. Is your house filled with fear? Fear not! Perfect love—*My love*—will chase fear away for good.

> Such love has no fear,
> because perfect love expels all fear.
> 1 John 4:18 NLT

13 Watching

I am watching over each moment of your life. No detail is too big or too small. So trust Me. Wait for Me. I am in control. Let Me lift the burden from your shoulders. *All is well.*

> With your unfailing love you lead the people
> you have redeemed.
> Exodus 15:13 NLT

14   Storms

Storms will come. When your heart belongs to Me, the enemy will try to attack. Outside the wind will blow, and the snow will fall. But inside—when you trust Me—the sun will shine on a quiet, happy heart filled with My peace.

He stilled the storm to a whisper.
Psalm 107:29

15   My Shadow

Does this day seem dark and covered in shadows? I have not left you. I am standing between you and your enemies. The shadows are Mine. They were sent to protect you. The sun will come back soon.

Those who live in the shelter of the Most High
will find rest in the shadow of the Almighty.
Psalm 91:1 NLT

16   Joy Again

You will know My joy again. Life—for now—is a long and difficult march. But it is a march you must make. So take your eyes off of your feet. Look ahead to My joy, and keep on marching.

Little children, let us not love in word or talk
but in deed and in truth.
1 John 3:18 ESV

17   Joy and Blessing

When the rain falls, everything and everyone gets wet. It doesn't mean I am angry. It doesn't mean I have taken My love away. Real joy and blessing can get soaking wet and still work just fine.

> The LORD has remembered us;
> he will bless us.
> Psalm 115:12 ESV

18   See My Wonders

Look around you. What do you see? Once upon a time this beautiful earth was just a dream in My heart. I spoke, and it appeared. I can do the same today. So tell Me—what dream is in your heart?

> You are the God of great wonders!
> Psalm 77:14 NLT

19 Perfect Love

Never let yourself fear anyone or anything. I will never fail you. I will never forget to take care of you. No matter what evil tries to surround you—trust Me and *fear not.*

I am surrounded by terror. My enemies conspire against me, plotting to take my life. But I am trusting you, O LORD.
Psalm 31:13–14 NLT

20 Fight Fear

Fight fear like your life depends on it. No matter how big or how small, every fear is working to cut the cords that tie you to My love. Don't be fooled by fear's tricks and lies. Trust Me. Fight back! *Fear not.*

Don't be afraid, for I am with you. Don't be discouraged, for I am your God.
Isaiah 41:10 NLT

21 Show Me Your Smile

I made every silver snowflake. I made each shining star. When life doesn't go the way you planned—be happy! Let Me see your beautiful smile. My love is watching over you. Everything will be all right.

I trust in your unfailing love.
I will rejoice because you have rescued me.
Psalm 13:5 NLT

22 Naturally

Fear not! I have conquered every evil. Nothing has the power to hurt you when you are hiding under My wings. Trust Me in the little things, and soon faith will come naturally in the big things.

He will cover you with his feathers,
and under his wings you will find refuge.
Psalm 91:4

23 The Path of Peace

Walk with Me on the path of peace. Let it be the wonderful fragrance of heaven that brings an unexpected blessing whenever you pass by.

Do all that you can to live in peace with everyone.
Romans 12:18 NLT

24 **Christ the Lord**

My Son is born—the Son of the One True God! Born not in a palace, but in a manger. Born not among kings, but among shepherds, sheep, and donkeys. Oh come, let us adore Him!

She will give birth to a son, and they will call him Immanuel, which means "God is with us."
Matthew 1:23 NLT

25 Babe of Bethlehem

Come. Kneel before the baby of Bethlehem.
Bring Him gifts of gold, frankincense, and myrrh.
Lay your wealth at His feet. Worship His name.
Share in His sorrow. My kingdom has come!

They opened their treasure chests and gave him
gifts of gold, frankincense, and myrrh.
Matthew 2:11 NLT

26 My Treasures

Walk My path, and give as you go. You will always
have enough. So take the next step, and don't be
afraid. I do not store up My treasures. I give them
freely and with joy. I want you to do the same.

We have left everything to follow you!
What then will there be for us?
Matthew 19:27

27

A New House

I have taken apart the house you built with selfishness and pride. Now build a new house, one brick at a time—with patience, kindness, and love—on the firm foundation of Jesus Christ.

My soul finds rest in God alone;
my salvation comes from him. He alone is my rock.
Psalm 62:1–2

28   Forever

I am here whether you feel Me or not. Feelings can
change with each breath of the wind. But I am not
changed by anything or anyone. I love you today.
I will love you tomorrow. I will love you *forever*.

He is the same yesterday, today, and forever.
Hebrews 13:8 CEV

29   Work and Prayer

Work and the prayers of a trusting heart are the
tools that will bring success. Go forward gladly,
and do not be afraid. The road ahead may look
difficult. But with Me, *all things* are possible.

With man this is impossible,
but with God all things are possible.
Matthew 19:26

30 Fishers of Men

Oh, how I cry over the pain of a lonely, broken heart. How it hurts to see My children trying to live without Me. Find them. Show them the way home. Open your heart, and bring them back to Me.

"Come, follow me," Jesus said,
"and I will make you fishers of men."
Mark 1:17

31 Jesus

My name is Jesus. I am the first and the last. The beginning and the end. There is no other name in heaven or earth by which you can be saved. I love you. I will take care of you. *You are Mine!*

You shall call his name Jesus. He will be great
and will be called the Son of the Most High. . .
and of his kingdom there will be no end.
Luke 1:31–33

Index

Index

Index

Index

Harmony

Index

PRAYER 1/6, 2/20, 27, 28, 3/23, 4/14, 5/14, 16, 26, 31, 8/2, 12, 10/19, 11/1, 27, 29, 12/29

RELAX 5/2

REST 1/21, 30, 3/17, 4/5, 15, 26, 5/8, 6/23, 8/6, 16, 9/15, 25

SAVED 7/13, 8/8

SECRET PLACE 3/16, 9/18, 10/15

Index

Index

write to **Phil A. Smouse**

Once upon a time, Phil A. Smouse wanted to be a scientist.

But scientists don't get wonderful letters and pictures from friends like you. So Phil decided to draw and color instead! He and his wife live in southwestern Pennsylvania. They have two children they love with all their heart.

Phil loves to tell kids like you all about Jesus. He would love to hear from you today! So get out your markers and crayons and send a letter or a picture to:

Phil A. Smouse
c/o Barbour Publishing, Inc.
P.O. Box 719
Uhrichsville, OH 44683

Or visit his website at http://www.philsmouse.com/
and send him an e-mail at: phil@philsmouse.com